# The Polar Bear

## Master of the Ice

Text by Valerie Tracqui

READER'S DIGEST

Animal Close-Ups

This edition is published by Reader's Digest Young Families, Inc.
Pleasantville, NY 10570
www.readersdigest.com

Copyright © Éditions Milan 1991. Toulouse, France.
Original edition first published by Éditions Milan under the title *l'ours blanc, seigneur de la banquise*
French series editor, Valérie Tracqui
Translated by Boston Language Institute

Copyright © 1994 in USA by Charlesbridge Publishing, Watertown, MA .

cover photo "© Alaska Stock/Tom Soucek 1999"

This huge male polar bear weighs almost 1,100 pounds. Its long, cat-like claws and strong sharp teeth are signs that it is a carnivore, a meat eater. It is the largest land carnivore in the world.

# Endless winter

A storm howls. Great gusts of wind blow over a landscape of ice and snow. Near the North Pole, in the area called the Arctic Circle, the sun never actually rises during late winter. The temperature goes down to 40° below zero, and the silvery ice seems to join with the sky.

In the distance, the huge shape of a polar bear appears like a ghost through the mists. Tired after its long trek, it stops to rest. Then, it moves on again southward, over the frozen sea. At times, the huge bear runs along at a speed of nearly 25 miles an hour. It roams a vast territory in search of food.

# Ready for the cold

Even in the freezing wind, the huge polar bear is perfectly comfortable. The long, white hairs of its thick fur let the sunlight pass right through them. This special type of fur lets the warmth of the sun reach the bear's black skin. The blinding glare of the sun on the white snow is not a problem for a polar bear. Its eyes are specially adapted to work like sunglasses and screen out the glare.

Its huge paws are as big as dinnerplates. The bottoms of the paws are insulated from the cold by short, stiff hairs that form a non-slip pad. Each toe has a long, black claw as sharp as an ice pick.

Polar bears have good balance. They can stand on their hind legs to look around or sniff the air.

Today, a heavy storm has made it difficult to find food, so the polar bear digs itself a shelter. It will stop to sleep for a few days.

Heavy, long, thick fur and a 4 inch layer of fat under its skin are very good protection from the cold.

Other adaptations are small ears that lose very little heat and no eyelashes which would freeze in icy storms.

The bottoms of its big, furry feet are like natural snowshoes. The polar bear does not need to worry about slipping on the ice.

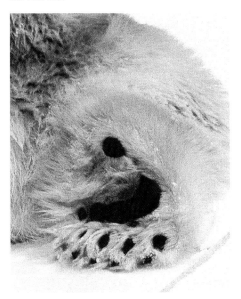

Very patiently, a polar bear waits for hours near a hole in the ice. Perhaps a seal will come up for air.

A seal weighing over 50 pounds would make a good meal for a polar bear.

This Arctic fox has followed the polar bear to find and eat any food the bear leaves behind.

# Hunting for seals

For five days the polar bear has not eaten, and it is very hungry. Suddenly it stops, its black nose twitching. It turns its head from side to side, catching the scent of a seal miles away. The hunt begins.

The polar bear climbs onto a floating piece of ice and then silently slips into the water, causing hardly a ripple. Between each piece of ice, it swims underwater. Each time it comes to the surface to breathe, it is a little closer to the seal. Suddenly, it comes up right beside the sleeping seal. With a single swipe of its paw, the hunt is over.

In the water, a seal can swim too fast for a polar bear to catch. Polar bears need to catch about one seal a week.

9

# A swimming champion

As winter comes to an end, the ice begins to break up. The polar bear does not worry about floating out to sea. It can swim for miles if it needs to. It can hold its breath underwater for several minutes, and its partly webbed paws make it a fast swimmer. When it decides to climb out onto the ice, it grips the ice with its sharp claws, using them like steel hooks.

When a wet polar bear hauls itself out of the water, it is a strange sight. Its narrow head, nine-foot-long body and small tail give it a streamlined shape for swimming.

In the water, the longer hairs of the polar bear's fur keep the thick fur beneath dry.

When swimming underwater, the polar bear closes its nostrils but keeps its eyes open.

When the polar bear climbs out of the icy water, it shakes like a dog. The water runs out of its fur before it freezes.

# Two baby bears

On a beautiful sunny day in March, two four-month-old polar bears come outdoors for the first time.

They were born in a den their mother dug in the snow. There they were sheltered from the wind and the cold. When spring arrived, the mother bear used her paws like snow shovels to reopen the tunnel doorway.

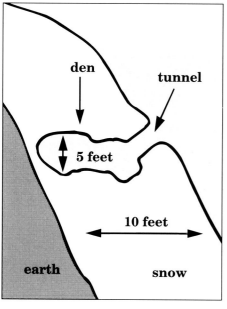

Baby polar bears are born in a snow cave called a den.

The mother polar bear did not sleep all winter. She hibernated by slowing down her breathing and dozing for about five months. Her heart beat slowed down, but her body temperature changed very little. She did not need to eat during her long nap because her layer of fat was her source of food.

In December, the mother polar bear gave birth to two tiny cubs. Newborn polar bear cubs weigh about as much as kittens, and like newborn kittens, their eyes are not open.

After a month, the cubs' eyes were open. They spent their days snuggling up against their mother for warmth and drinking her milk.

When they finally leave the den, the cubs weigh about 20 to 30 pounds.

The polar bear cubs drink their mother's milk until they are one and a half years old. The cubs will stay with their mother until they are two years old.

Each day, the mother takes her cubs out to explore. There is much to see and many lessons to learn.

Always playful, the cubs often frolic with their mother. Each night, they return to the safety of their den.

During the spring, the family begins a long trip across the ice.

# Family life

The curious cubs watch carefully everything their mother does. They play games together, rolling, climbing, and sliding on the snow. After a few weeks, the mother is so hungry that she must leave the den and head for the seal-hunting grounds.

The cubs bravely follow their mother across miles of ice. The mother stops often so her babies can have a drink and take a nap. She sniffs the air for the smell of danger. Prowling wolf packs look for easy prey such as bear cubs. For the moment, everything is fine. The mother gives a few grunts to tell the cubs that it is time to move on.

# Water games

After they learn how to swim, polar bears love to play in the water. Even on their first day in the water, they begin to play games that test their strength and develop their coordination.

Although they will rarely fight when they are grown, young bears often play by pretending to fight each other.

The playmates are careful not to hurt each other.

Each one tries to splash and knock down the other cub.

The bigger the cubs get, the more fun their water sports become. These two have rolled off the ice into the water!

Roaring and hissing and showing your teeth — all part of the game.

Slowly turning together in the water, one cub nips at his sister's nose. She kicks her brother away. Then they give each other a big bear hug!

# A brief encounter

It is now May, the time when male and female polar bears meet to mate. Drawn by her scent, two males approach a female. This female has no cubs to care for.

The two males lower their heads menacingly and turn to face each other. Then the contest begins. With the hair on their backs standing straight up, they begin circling each other, grunting out warnings. They wrestle until the weaker of the two acknowledges the strength of his rival and leaves. The winner will spend only about a week with the female before he leaves to hunt for food.

Standing on his hind legs, a male polar bear is tall enough to look an elephant in the eye. He may weigh as much as 1,500 pounds.

Polar bear mothers take care of their cubs for two years. The mother can have a new pair of cubs every 3 years.

18

When mating time is over, the males go off to live alone. They will not be able to recognize their own cubs if they should ever meet them.

Mother polar bear teaches her cubs how to hunt small rodents, called lemmings.

Hungry polar bears will eat moss, lichen, leaves, and berries.

Even though white fur in the snow is excellent camouflage, the arctic hare cannot hide from a polar bear's powerful sense of smell.

Polar bears like to stay clean. After eating, mother bear shows her cubs the proper way to use one's paws to wash, just like a cat.

# On the tundra

Summer is coming. The sun looks like a big red circle on the horizon. The ice is breaking up into pieces that drift out to sea. Mother bear must either lead her cubs north, following the seals, or teach the cubs how to get food on the tundra. She chooses the tundra.

In summer on the tundra, polar bears become omnivores, eating anything they can find. They eat bird eggs and hatchlings, fish, rodents, lichen, seaweed, and berries. Frequent plunges in the nearby water help them to cool off.

Young Arctic foxes wait for the polar bear's leftovers.

# The cubs grow up

After two months on the tundra, mother polar bear knows that soon winter will begin. The first sign is ice around the edge of the bay. Then the waters freeze and again become a solid sheet of ice. At last, the seals return.

This winter the mother and her cubs do not stay in a den. They hunt seals all winter. They curl up together during storms and let the falling snow be their blanket. In the spring, the mother says goodbye to the cubs, and they go off on their own. They do not need her help and protection anymore.

The cubs are two years old when they leave their mother. They stay together for a few weeks before they decide to leave each other, too.

# Polar bears and people

For two hundred years, polar bears were killed for their fur. Today they're protected by an international treaty. Slowly, their numbers have increased, but now a new menace threatens their safety: pollution.

In trying to find food in the autumn, polar bears sometimes visit dumps, where they may be harmed by eating poisonous chemicals.

## An Inuit spirit
For thousands of years, the Inuit (Eskimos) worshipped the polar bear as a spirit. It was bad luck to anger "Nanouk," as the Inuit called the bear spirit. They hunted the polar bear with great skill. They ate its meat and used its fur to make parkas, shoes, and leggings.

## Hunted for 200 years
It is thought that polar bears lived in the Arctic for fifty to eighty thousand years before the arrival of the first whaling vessels in the 1600's. Then, for the next two hundred years, non-native hunters brought guns to the Arctic and killed thousands of polar bears each year. The bears were killed only for their fur and for sport.

## Protected at last
Finally, international cooperation was necessary to adequately protect this endangered species. In 1965, every nation bordering the arctic decided to ban the hunting of polar bear mothers and their cubs. The polar bear is still on the international list of endangered species.

In order to study a polar bear, scientists first tranquilize it so they can weigh and examine it.

## At the crossroads

In 1974, a treaty was signed by the five countries bordering the Arctic. It banned the capture of polar bears, except by scientists working to preserve the species, and by Inuit, who are allowed to hunt only a certain number every year.

Five nations are involved with the protection of polar bears.

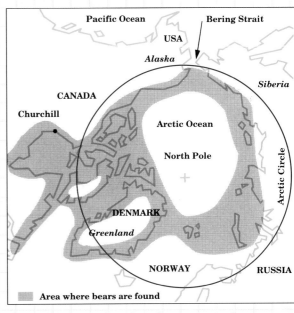

A map of polar bear territory

Each year, the Inuit are allowed to hunt some polar bears in Alaska and some in Greenland.

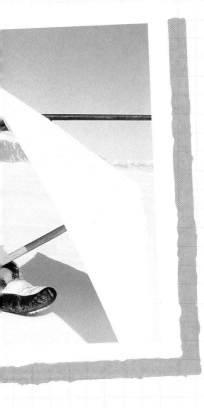

## Game preserves

The treaty of 1976 called for the five nations to protect the polar bear's feeding and breeding grounds and their migration routes. Today, the polar bear population is slowly recovering. In certain areas where polar bears are plentiful, a thriving tourist industry has arisen. The town of Churchill, Manitoba on Hudson Bay, has become "the polar bear capital of Canada."

## The pollution threat

Even if there isn't much risk of being hunted anymore, polar bears still face another threat: pollution. Researchers have found pesticides and dangerous metals in the bodies of both polar bears and seals. Increasing development of natural resources such as oil also threaten their fragile environment. A single oil tanker accident could have catastrophic consequences.

# Other kinds of bears

The bear family includes seven species. The three largest are the brown bear, the black bear and the polar bear. These three bears are the largest carnivores on the face of the earth.

The American Black Bear includes 18 sub-species which have a variety of colors. It is smaller than the brown bear and has shorter hair and claws. The claws are sharp enough to quickly climb trees. More timid than the brown bear and native to a wider geographic area, it usually doesn't bother people.

The European Brown Bear lives in forests, plains and mountains and is a good tree climber. It usually hunts at night. Because there are only a few left in France, there is a real danger that this bear might disappear entirely. Brown bears are protected by law, but they suffer from battles with wild pigs, a shrinking forest, and the growing presence of tourists.

▼

◄ The Grizzly Bear is an American sub-species of brown bear. Larger than its European cousin, it is quite impressive when rearing up on its hind legs to better observe an unfamiliar object or person. It can be found in national parks where it is protected and in less developed parts of Canada and Alaska. Along the rivers, grizzlies fish for salmon. Sometimes several grizzlies can be seen in the same area fishing.

# For Further Reading...

Horton, Casey. *Endangered! Bears.* New York: Marshall Cavendish, 1996.

Lepthien, Emilie. *Polar Bears.* A New True Book. Chicago: Childrens Press, 1991.

Matthews, Downs. *Polar Bear Cubs.* Photographs by Dan Guravich. New York: Simon and Schuster Books for Young Readers, 1989.

# To See Polar Bears in Captivity...

Many zoos also have web sites on the internet. To learn more about their exhibits, go to the following page on the Yahoo WWW site:
**http://www.yahoo.com/science/biology/zoology/zoos**

# Use the Internet to Find Out More About Polar Bears...

*Seaworld/Busch Gardens: Polar Bears.* Lots of information with a great index.
**http://www/seaworld.org/polar_bears/pbindex.html**

*Polar Bears Alive.* A great photo gallery.
**http://www.polarbearsalive.org/gallery.htm**

*Zoobooks.* Pet a polar bear!
**http://www.zoobooks.com/petp.htm**

*The Polar Bear and the Walrus.* Make a blubber mitten.
**http://www.teelfamily.com/activities/polarbear/**